LINCOLN Tells a Joke

HOW LAUGHTER SAVED THE PRESIDENT (AND THE COUNTRY)

Kathleen Krull & Paul Brewer

ILLUSTRATED BY Stacy Innerst

Clarion Books
An Imprint of HarperCollins*Publishers*
Boston New York

POOR
Abraham
Lincoln.

His life was hardly fun at all.

His childhood was harsh.

He looked homely and he knew it.

Sadness disturbed him off and on.

His family had ups and downs.

When he ran for public office, he often lost.

As our sixteenth president, he was unpopular.

And when his country went to war,

it nearly split in two.

But Lincoln had his own way of dealing with life.

Not many people remember it today.

It was all about laughing.

Ha

Ha

ha

ha

Ha

HA

Ha

HA

a

HA

Ha

H ra

HA

Lincoln was born in a log cabin in 1809, which might sound cool, but it was actually quite bleak. The floor was made of dirt, the beds were piles of cornhusks, and snow blew in through cracks in the walls. Life on the frontier—first in Kentucky, then in Indiana—was almost all work. Backbreaking work.

Lincoln's father was strict during the workday, but at night he told jokes and the family laughed together. *"My father taught me how to work, but not to love it,"* Lincoln said later. *"I'd rather read, tell stories, crack jokes, talk, laugh."*

All his life he liked to read aloud to hear the sound of the words. Words were like magic. At seven he learned to write them, and he later kept a scrapbook of favorite words. When paper was scarce he wrote on boards, in the snow, in the dusty earth. Most of his neighbors couldn't read or write, and sometimes they hired him to write letters for them.

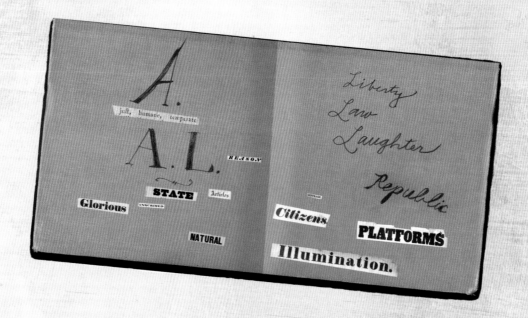

When Lincoln was nine, his mother died. He helped build her coffin, so sad he couldn't even speak her name.

Words and humor seemed to ease the pain. On Sundays he and his friends would go off into the woods, where he would stand on a tree stump and read aloud from *Quinn's Jests*. He was also fond of a book called *Lessons in Elocution* and followed its advice about how to speak in a way that made people want to listen.

He wrote his first nonsense poem at age eleven.

Abraham Lincoln
His hand and pen
He will be good but
God knows when

Lincoln was crazy about learning, but because he was always needed to work at home, he had a total of only one year of official schooling.

By the time he turned seventeen, his rail-thin frame had grown to six feet, four inches. He had huge hands, huge feet, and a huge nose. But he wasn't embarrassed. He poked fun at his looks instead.

Lincoln left home when he was nineteen, after the death of his beloved sister. He worked at numerous tough jobs, always with a book in his back pocket. He read anytime he could.

In the evenings, he liked to swap jokes and stories with folks at the general store in New Salem, Illinois. The local judge found him so amusing that he invited him to court to comment on current cases.

There Lincoln saw that the power of words could put someone in jail or free them. Words mattered. Not that there wasn't foolishness in court. He said of a lawyer who irked him, *"That man can pack the most words into the least ideas of any man I know."*

Lincoln served three months in the military when he was twenty-three. The men in his company elected him captain, but there wasn't much fighting to oversee.

He would joke that he survived *"a good many bloody battles—with mosquitoes."*

That same year, he ran for the Illinois state legislature. He loved to laugh, but he was also intensely ambitious. One of his campaign tactics was telling jokes.

He lost.

Two years later, he ran for office again, and by this time voters took him more seriously. He was elected to the Illinois House of Representatives, where he served four terms, still joking. "He kept the House in a continuous roar of merriment," said an admirer.

Lincoln continued to make fun of his own appearance, saying, *"Common-looking people are the best in the world; that is the reason the Lord makes so many of them."* By now he had a wart on his cheek, a scar over one eye, and many bad hair days. He often looked moody and withdrawn, but when he told a joke, his expression would change completely.

His early romances ended tragically. He had frequent insomnia and nightmares. Yet he could still laugh—and people noticed that children who hung around him were always laughing, too.

He could cheer up a neighbor, saying, *"It's a great day for the race."*

"What race?" the neighbor would ask.

"The human race!"

In his free time, Lincoln studied to become a lawyer. He was terrible at keeping track of his papers. He labeled a teetering pile in his office with a sign:

WHEN YOU CAN'T FIND IT ANYWHERE ELSE, LOOK IN THIS.

But he succeeded at putting his talent for words to work. In the courthouses around Springfield he was brilliant, reducing hours of argument into one clever story that would get the jury on his side.

After Lincoln met Mary Todd, he learned that she hated slavery, just as he did. She was witty, bubbly, and very smart about politics. Her wealthy, snobbish family felt he was not quite her equal, and they disapproved. But even then he could joke. *"One d is enough for God, but the Todds need two,"* he wrote sarcastically to a friend.

He and Mary finally married. His moodiness sometimes drove her into a rage, but they were devoted to each other. Sixteen inches taller than Mary, he often joked about the difference in their heights. He would address a crowd from a balcony: *"Here I am, and here is Mrs. Lincoln. And that's the long and short of it."*

The Lincolns had four boys: Robert, Eddie, Willie, and Tad. Lincoln was such a playful father that some frowned, but he believed a good sense of humor made children smarter. He thought jokes should be taught in schools, just like reading, writing, and arithmetic.

After Eddie died at age three and Willie at age twelve, it took Lincoln a long time to laugh again.

Lincoln wanted to fix things he saw wrong in the country, so he kept running for higher office. Telling a joke was a way to get people to listen, to like him— and to vote for him.

He wrote comical letters to newspapers, mocking his opponents. An outstanding mimic, he once imitated a rival so perfectly that the other man cried. Lincoln felt bad about that and apologized later.

He had some embarrassing election losses, but many people came to respect his honesty. *"You may fool all of the people some of the time,"* he said. *"You can even fool some of the people all of the time. But you can't fool all of the people all of the time."*

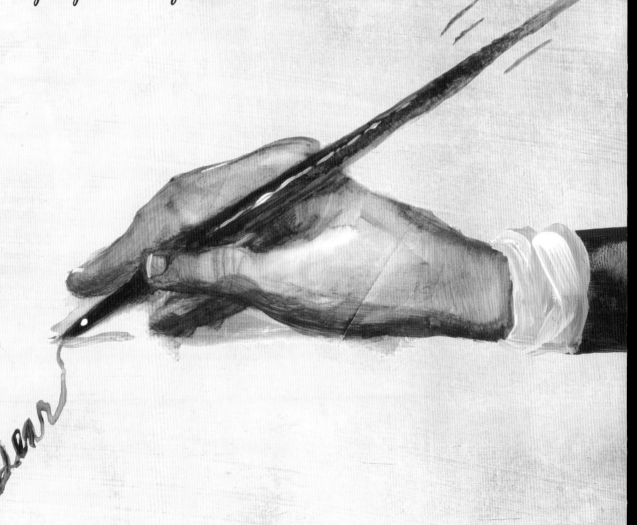

When no ladies were around, he might joke about farts or outhouses. But he could be witty even about the most serious subjects: *"Whenever I hear anyone arguing for slavery, I feel a strong impulse to see it tried on him personally."*

He knew, too, that sometimes it's best not to joke: *"Better to remain silent and be thought a fool than to speak out and remove all doubt."*

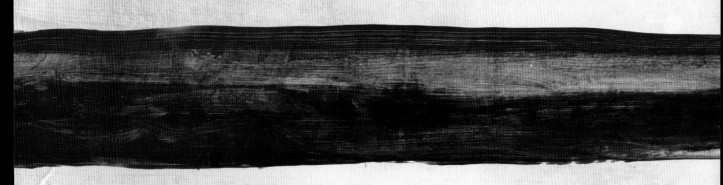

Abraham Lincoln was elected president in 1860, to the surprise of those who lacked a sense of humor.

In Washington, D.C., he often spent the days receiving visitors in his office. He kept books of jokes in his desk drawer. *"That reminds me of a leetle story,"* he would say, cackling, then dazzle his guest. He laughed more than anyone at his own stories, letting it all out with a mighty **"HEE HEE!"** in his high-pitched voice, grasping his knees and rocking back and forth. The former president Martin Van Buren declared that his "sides were sore with laughing" after an evening with Lincoln.

Lincoln firmly believed that jokes added sweetening when he had to break bad news, scold someone, give orders he knew would be hard, or get along with difficult people. A funny story was also a way of stalling when he was asked for secret information. The visitor would leave laughing, only later realizing that the president had revealed nothing of importance.

Lincoln was often asked for favors, and he felt bad when he refused. When he came down with a mild case of contagious smallpox, he quipped, *"Well, I've got something now that I can give to everybody!"*

His jokes did offend some proper folks. They thought the president couldn't be both funny and smart. A popular song ridiculed him for acting like a clown: **"HEY, UNCLE ABE, ARE YOU JOKING YET?"**

The Civil War broke out only a month after Abraham Lincoln became president.

The country fought about slavery and the rights of states. Communities, even families, fell apart. Other politicians had failed to forge a compromise.

It was the worst crisis since the country was born. The
United States, united no more, was in danger of splitting
into two countries, one north, one south.

The war continued for four miserable years—620,000
boys and men died, someone from nearly every family.

Lincoln aged rapidly during these years and looked much older than he really was. But once again, laughter often helped him. Before he made difficult decisions, he read funny passages aloud from his favorite humor writers, telling his advisors, *"With the fearful strain that is upon me night and day, if I did not laugh occasionally I should die, and you need this medicine as much as I do."*

In cabinet meetings, he would beg, *"Gentlemen, why don't you laugh?"*

Four score and seven
brought forth, upon th
ceived in Liberty and
that all men
Now we are
And so
here on a
come to de
that

Against the odds, Lincoln kept the North and South together, partly because of his serious, brilliant speeches. He spent days writing those speeches, showing his ear for rhythm and just the right word. He was a master of grammar. His gift for language—and how it can inspire people—is one reason he is considered one of our best presidents.

But at the time, he was the most unpopular president ever, due to his politics, not his jokes. He received thousands of death threats. Yet he could make light even of these, saying that the first few made him *"a little uncomfortable, but there is nothing like getting used to things!"*

Five days after the war finally ended in 1865, the Lincolns attended a performance of a popular comic play. The laughter of the audience covered the sound of a gun being fired behind the president. It's possible that Lincoln was laughing even in the final moments of his life. He died at age fifty-six, and never saw the rebirth of his united country.

Yet Abraham Lincoln had kept Americans together,
thanks to the love of laughter that kept him going,
step by step, on a journey that took him
all the way to the White House and into history.

For Brad Horwitz and Jana Carlson —K.K. ✢ P.B.

For Susan —S.I.

A Note from the Authors:

Lincoln's jokes in this book are from collections compiled by a variety of people,
often after his death. Some of his clever remarks were passed on by eyewitnesses; some are
second-hand, third-hand, or further removed. For links to his famous serious words, visit
www.lincolnbicentennial.gov/lincolns-life/words-and-speeches.

Sources

De Regniers, Beatrice Schenk. *The Abraham Lincoln Joke Book*. New York: Scholastic, 1965.

Donald, David Herbert. *We Are Lincoln Men: Abraham Lincoln and His Friends*. New York:
Simon & Schuster, 2003.

———. *Lincoln*. New York: Simon & Schuster, 1995.

Freedman, Russell. *Lincoln: A Photobiography*. New York: Clarion Books, 1987.

Herbert, Janis. *Abraham Lincoln for Kids: His Life and Times with 21 Activities*. Chicago:
Chicago Review Press, 2007.

Holzer, Harold, ed. *Lincoln as I Knew Him: Gossip, Tributes, and Revelations from His Best Friends and
Worst Enemies*. Chapel Hill, N.C.: Algonquin Books, 1999.

Lincoln Bicentennial. www.lincolnbicentennial.gov/default.aspx.

McClure, Alexander. *"Abe" Lincoln's Yarns and Stories*. Philadelphia: International
Publishing Company, 1901.

Rice, Allen Thorndike, ed. *Reminiscences of Abraham Lincoln by Distinguished Men of His Time*.
New York: North American Review, 1888.

Stein, Max. *Abe Lincoln's Jokes*. 1943.

Zall, P. M., ed. *Abe Lincoln Laughing: Humorous Anecdotes from Original Sources by and About Abraham
Lincoln*. Knoxville: University of Tennessee Press, 1995.

The illustrations in this book were done in acrylic on illustration board.
The text type was set in Civil War Type No. 1.
The display type was set in Civil War Type No. 11, Civil War Type No. 12, and Handsome Classic.
Designed by Sara Gillingham

The Library of Congress has cataloged the hardcover edition as follows:
Krull, Kathleen.
Lincoln tells a joke : how laughter saved the president (and the country) / Kathleen Krull and Paul Brewer ; illustrated by Stacy Innerst.
p. cm.
Includes bibliographical references.
1. Lincoln, Abraham, 1809–1865—Juvenile literature. 2. Presidents—United States—Biography—Juvenile literature. 3. Joking—United States—
History—19th century—Juvenile literature. 4. Laughter—United States—History—19th century—Juvenile literature. 5. Laughter—Political
aspects—United States—History—19th century—Juvenile literature. 6. Humor in the workplace—United States—History—19th century—
Juvenile literature. 7. United States—History—Civil War, 1861–1865—Juvenile literature. I. Brewer, Paul, 1950– II. Innerst, Stacy, ill. III. Title.
E457.905.K78 2010
973.7092—dc22
[B]
2009024197

ISBN: 978-0-15-206639-0 hardcover
ISBN: 978-0-544-66828-7 paperback

Manufactured in China
22 SCP 15 14 13 12 11 10 9 8 7